21042

Team Spirit

THE BALTIMORE ORIOLES

BY

MARK STEWART

Content Consultant
James L. Gates, Jr.
Library Director
National Baseball Hall of Fame and Museum

NORWOOD HOUSE PRESS

CHICAGO, ILLINOIS

Norwood House Press
P.O. Box 316598
Chicago, Illinois 60631

For information regarding Norwood House Press, please visit our website at:
www.norwoodhousepress.com or call 866-565-2900.

All photos courtesy of AP Images—AP/Wide World Photos, Inc., except the following:
Author's Collection (6, 36, 41 left);
Topps, Inc. (7, 14, 16, 21 top & bottom, 22, 29, 30, 34 all, 37 bottom, 40 both, 41 bottom right);
John Klein (8, 9, 23 top, 26, 31, 38, 43); Golden Press (20).
Special thanks to Topps, Inc.

Editor: Mike Kennedy
Designer: Ron Jaffe
Project Management: Black Book Partners, LLC.

Library of Congress Cataloging-in-Publication Data

Stewart, Mark, 1960-
   The Baltimore Orioles / by Mark Stewart ; content consultant James L.
Gates, Jr.
      p. cm. -- (Team spirit)
   Summary: "Presents the history, accomplishments and key personalities of
the Baltimore Orioles baseball team. Includes timelines, quotes, maps,
glossary and website"--Provided by publisher.
   Includes bibliographical references and index.
   ISBN-13: 978-1-59953-092-5 (library edition : alk. paper)
   ISBN-10: 1-59953-092-9 (library edition : alk. paper)
   1. Baltimore Orioles (Baseball team)--Juvenile literature. I. Gates, Jr.,
James L. II. Title.
GV875.B2S74 2007
796.357'64097526--dc22
                                        2006033022

COVER PHOTO: Luis Matos, Melvin Mora, and Jay Gibbons congratulate each other after a victory by the Orioles.

Table of Contents

CHAPTER	PAGE
Meet the Orioles	4
Way Back When	6
The Team Today	10
Home Turf	12
Dressed for Success	14
We Won!	16
Go-To Guys	20
On the Sidelines	24
One Great Day	26
Legend Has It	28
It Really Happened	30
Team Spirit	32
Timeline	34
Fun Facts	36
Talking Baseball	38
For the Record	40
Pinpoints	42
Play Ball	44
Glossary	46
Places to Go	47
Index	48

SPORTS WORDS & VOCABULARY WORDS: In this book, you will find many words that are new to you. You may also see familiar words used in new ways. The glossary on page 46 gives the meanings of baseball words, as well as "everyday" words that have special baseball meanings. These words appear in **bold type** throughout the book. The glossary on page 47 gives the meanings of vocabulary words that are not related to baseball. They appear in ***bold italic type*** throughout the book.

Meet the Orioles

The Baltimore oriole is a bird with a lot of personality. Each sings a slightly different tune, and defends its territory with bravery and intelligence. In many places, the bird's arrival means that spring has come. All of these things could be said of the Baltimore Orioles baseball team, too.

The Orioles always seem to have players with strong personalities. Some are quiet leaders, while others like to make noise and joke around. Every player, however, takes the game very seriously.

This book tells the story of the Orioles. The team is known for giving opportunities to young players, and for paying close attention to the **fundamentals**. Some of the greatest stars in history have played for the Orioles, and many of baseball's most amazing moments have happened with the Orioles on the field.

Nick Markakis and Brian Roberts, two young Orioles who brought Baltimore fans to the ballpark in 2006.

Way Back When

The story of the Orioles begins in the city of St. Louis, Missouri. In 1901, a new league—the **American League (A.L.)**—rose up to challenge the older **National League (N.L.)**. One year later, the A.L. placed a team in St. Louis to compete with the Cardinals, and called it the Browns. They finished second in their first season, and the future looked bright.

The Browns had many good hitters over the years, including Bobby Wallace, George Sisler, Del Pratt, Ken Williams, Jack Tobin, and Harlond Clift. However, the team would finish better than second just once in 52 seasons. Their only **pennant** came in 1944. By then, the Browns had started thinking about finding a new home. After the 1953 season, they moved to Baltimore, Maryland, and were renamed the Orioles.

WALLACE, ST. LOUIS, AMER.

The Orioles lost 100 games in 1954, but the losing would not last long. The team spent a lot of money and time developing new players. Baltimore's first big star was Brooks Robinson. He was the best fielding third baseman anyone had ever seen. Robinson could hit, too. In 1964, Robinson led the A.L. in **runs batted in (RBIs)** and was named the league's **Most Valuable Player (MVP)**.

BROOKS ROBINSON
Third Base

Baltimore
Orioles

Robinson was joined by other good, young players in the 1960s, including Boog Powell, Paul Blair, Milt Pappas, Steve Barber, Wally Bunker, Jim Palmer, and Dave McNally. By 1966, the team had added **All-Stars** Frank Robinson and Luis Aparicio to the **lineup**. The Orioles won the pennant and defeated the Los Angeles Dodgers in the **World Series** that season. In 1968, Baltimore hired a *feisty* manager named Earl Weaver. He won four more pennants over the next 12 years.

By the 1980s, the names and faces had changed in Baltimore, but the winning *tradition* continued. The club was now led by

LEFT: Bobby Wallace was the Browns' first star.
ABOVE: Brooks Robinson was a good hitter and a great fielder.

young superstars Cal Ripken Jr. and Eddie Murray. Ripken would become one of the greatest and most popular players in history. From 1982 to 1998, he played in 2,632 games in a row.

In 1992, the Orioles moved into beautiful new Oriole Park at Camden Yards. More than two million people a year came to watch the team play. They rooted for Ripken and his talented teammates, including Mike Mussina, Roberto Alomar, Rafael Palmeiro, Brady Anderson, Scott Erickson, and Randy Myers. In 1996 and 1997, the Orioles reached the **American League Championship Series (ALCS)**, but could not take the final step needed to win another pennant. After Ripken retired in 2001, the team began a new chapter in its great history.

LEFT: Cal Ripken Jr., the greatest player in Baltimore history.
ABOVE: Roberto Alomar led the Orioles to the ALCS twice in the 1990s.

The Team Today

The Orioles play in a ballpark that is very good for hitters. The team tries to take advantage of this by finding powerful **sluggers**, and then surrounding them with players who are good at getting on base. Baltimore fans, meanwhile, have always loved young, hard-throwing pitchers who challenge opponents to hit the ball. These are the type of pitchers the Orioles still try to sign.

The Orioles are a fun team to watch because of the way they mix young players with experienced stars. The older Orioles teach the younger ones, while the younger ones get the crowd excited with their enthusiasm.

Almost every season, Baltimore fans have an exciting new Oriole to root for. In recent years, they have cheered on Brian Roberts, Nick Markakis, and Erik Bedard. The Orioles are counting on players like these to become All-Stars and lead the team to the top of the **standings**.

Melvin Mora gets a "high-five" from Brian Roberts after scoring a run.

Home Turf

For their first 38 seasons, the Orioles played in Baltimore's Memorial Stadium. In 1992, the team moved into Oriole Park at Camden Yards—or simply "Camden Yards," as fans now call it. The stadium is just two blocks from the birthplace of Babe Ruth, who grew up in Baltimore and played for an early **minor-league** team called the Orioles. Ruth's father ran a café on Conway Street, which is now part of the center field stands.

The company that created Camden Yards studied baseball's most famous ballparks, including Wrigley Field, Fenway Park, Ebbets Field, and the Polo Grounds. The builders mixed the best of these old stadiums with many new ideas. Since Camden Yards opened, several other teams have built stadiums mixing old and new.

CAMDEN YARDS BY THE NUMBERS

- *There are 48,262 seats in Oriole Park at Camden Yards.*
- *The right field wall is 25 feet high, while the wall in left field is only seven feet high.*
- *The distance from home plate to the left field foul pole is 333 feet.*
- *The distance from home plate to the center field fence is 400 feet.*
- *The distance from home plate to the right field foul pole is 318 feet.*

There is plenty of history and lots of action for the fans at Camden Yards.

Dressed for Success

The Orioles have always worn black and orange, the colors of the bird for which they were named. The team has used an oriole on its cap every season, though for a short while in the 1960s they switched to an orange letter "B" for hats worn at home games.

In some years, the Orioles' cap *logo* has looked like a real bird. In others, it has been a cartoon oriole. Several different artists have drawn Baltimore's oriole, including Jim Hartzell, Hal Decker, and Stan Walsh. Walsh was famous for creating the breakfast cereal characters Snap, Crackle, and Pop.

The team has worn many different uniforms over the years, but always with the color combination of orange, black, and white. In the early 1970s, the Orioles sometimes wore orange bottoms and tops at the same time!

Billy Loes poses in the team's road uniform of the 1950s.

UNIFORM BASICS

The baseball uniform has not changed much since the Orioles began playing. It has four main parts:

- a cap or batting helmet with a sun visor
- a top with a player's number on the back
- pants that reach down between the ankle and the knee
- stirrup-style socks

The uniform top sometimes has a player's name on the back. The team's name, city, or logo is usually on the front. Baseball teams wear light-colored uniforms when they play at home, and darker styles when they play on the road.

For more than 100 years, baseball uniforms were made of wool *flannel* and were very baggy. This helped the sweat *evaporate* and gave players the freedom to move around. Today's uniforms are made of *synthetic* fabrics that stretch with players and keep them dry and cool.

Corey Patterson models the team's 2006 uniform, with "Orioles" written in script across the front.

We Won!

The difference between a good team and a championship team can be a single player. That was the case in 1966, when the Orioles traded for Frank Robinson. Baltimore already had excellent pitching, speed, and defense, but needed one more big bat in the lineup. Robinson gave the team the help it needed by winning the **Triple Crown** and MVP award. He teamed up with Boog Powell and Brooks Robinson to hit more than 100 home runs, and the Orioles won the pennant by nine games.

That year, the Orioles faced the Los Angeles Dodgers in the World Series. Most fans thought the Dodgers would win. They had two of the best pitchers in baseball, Sandy Koufax and Don Drysdale. In Game One, the Orioles scored four runs in the first two innings against Drysdale. When the Dodgers scored twice to make the score 4–2, Baltimore manager Hank Bauer brought in a **relief pitcher** named Moe Drabowsky in the third inning. Drabowsky finished the game and struck out 11 batters. The Orioles won 5–2.

Amazingly, the Dodgers would not score again. The next afternoon, 20-year-old Jim Palmer beat Koufax 6–0. Two days later, in Baltimore, Wally Bunker took the mound for the Orioles and **shut out** Los Angeles 1–0. Dave McNally finished off the Dodgers in Game Four with another 1–0 shutout, and the Orioles had their first championship.

LEFT: Frank Robinson, who won the Triple Crown and MVP in 1966.
ABOVE: Brooks Robinson and Andy Etchebarren hug Dave McNally after winning the 1966 World Series. Boog Powell is about to join the celebration.

Baltimore won more than 100 games and returned to the World Series each year from 1969 to 1971. The Orioles lost to the New York Mets in '69 and the Pittsburgh Pirates in '71, but they defeated the Cincinnati Reds in 1970. Brooks Robinson was the star of this series. He made one great fielding play after another, and batted .429. Another Oriole who had a great series was McNally. He threw a **complete game** and hit the first **grand slam** by a pitcher in a World Series. The Orioles beat Cincinnati four games to one.

The Orioles lost a rematch with the Pirates in the 1979 World Series, but returned to play in the 1983 World Series against the Philadelphia Phillies. After losing Game One, Baltimore won comeback victories in the next three games, and then beat the Phillies 5–0 in Game Five for the team's third championship. The pitching stars included Scott McGregor, Mike Flanagan, Mike Boddicker, Tippy Martinez, and Palmer—the same player who had beaten the Dodgers 17 years earlier! The man calling the pitches for the Orioles, catcher Rick Dempsey, was chosen as World Series MVP.

ABOVE: Brooks Robinson makes a diving catch in the 1970 World Series.   **RIGHT**: Rick Dempsey waves his cap during the Orioles' victory parade in 1983.

Go-To Guys

To be a true star in baseball, you need more than a quick bat and a strong arm. You have to be a "go-to guy"—someone the manager wants on the pitcher's mound or in the batter's box when it matters most. Fans of the Browns and Orioles have had a lot to cheer about over the years, including these great stars…

THE PIONEERS

GEORGE SISLER — First Baseman

• BORN: 3/24/1893 • DIED: 3/26/1973 • PLAYED FOR TEAM: 1915 TO 1927

George Sisler was a great college pitcher when he joined the Browns, but his hitting was so good that the team moved him to first base. He won two batting championships and led the A.L. in stolen bases four times.

GEORGE SISLER
first base

KEN WILLIAMS — Outfielder

• BORN: 6/28/1890 • DIED: 1/22/1959
• PLAYED FOR TEAM: 1918 TO 1927

Ken Williams was a fast and powerful outfielder. In 1922, he hit 39 home runs and stole 37 bases for the Browns. This made Williams the first member of the "30–30" club.

ABOVE: George Sisler
TOP RIGHT: Brooks Robinson **BOTTOM RIGHT**: Frank Robinson

BROOKS ROBINSON — Third Baseman

- BORN: 5/18/1937
- PLAYED FOR TEAM: 1955 TO 1977

Brooks Robinson was the starting third baseman in the All-Star Game 15 years in a row. He was such a good fielder that he was nicknamed the "human vacuum cleaner." Robinson was A.L. MVP in 1964, All-Star Game MVP in 1966, and World Series MVP in 1970.

JIM PALMER — Pitcher

- BORN: 10/15/1945
- PLAYED FOR TEAM: 1965 TO 1967 & 1969 TO 1984

Jim Palmer overcame control problems and a sore arm to win the **Cy Young Award** three times for the Orioles in the 1970s. His high leg-kick and over-the-top throwing style helped him win 20 or more games eight times between 1970 and 1978.

FRANK ROBINSON — Outfielder

- BORN: 8/31/1935   • PLAYED FOR TEAM: 1966 TO 1971

The Cincinnati Reds traded Frank Robinson to the Orioles because they thought he was too old. Robinson proved them wrong by winning the Triple Crown in his first season with Baltimore, and leading the team to its first championship. He hit 179 home runs during his six years as an Oriole.

MODERN STARS

MIKE FLANAGAN
Pitcher

• BORN: 12/16/1951   • PLAYED FOR TEAM: 1975 TO 1987 & 1991 TO 1992

Mike Flanagan was one of baseball's most dependable players. Between 1977 and 1987, no pitcher in the A.L. started more games. Flanagan had a marvelous curveball, and specialized in picking off runners who wandered too far from first base.

EDDIE MURRAY
First Baseman/Designated Hitter

• BORN: 2/24/1956   • PLAYED FOR TEAM: 1977 TO 1988 & 1996

Eddie Murray was the most fearsome **switch-hitter** of his day. He was at his best with runners on base, and especially dangerous with the bases loaded. Murray also won the **Gold Glove** three times for his excellent fielding.

EDDIE MURRAY

CAL RIPKEN JR.
Shortstop/ Third Baseman

• BORN: 8/24/1960

• PLAYED FOR TEAM: 1981 TO 2001

Cal Ripken Jr. was the heart and soul of the Orioles for two *decades*. He won two MVP awards and finished his career with more than 3,000 hits and 400 home runs.

MIKE MUSSINA   **Pitcher**

- BORN: 12/8/1968   • PLAYED FOR TEAM: 1991 TO 2000

Mike Mussina used a darting fastball and a strange "knuckle-curve" to become the team's best pitcher in the 1990s. He won 147 games for the Orioles, and led Baltimore in victories in six seasons.

MELVIN MORA   **Third Baseman**

- BORN: 2/2/1972

- FIRST YEAR WITH TEAM: 2000

In his first four seasons with the Orioles, Melvin Mora played every position except pitcher and catcher. No matter where he lined up in the field, Mora always did well in the batter's box. In 2004, he set a record for the Orioles with a .340 batting average.

MIGUEL TEJADA   **Shortstop**

- BORN: 5/25/1976   • FIRST YEAR WITH TEAM: 2004

Baltimore fans were thrilled when the team announced it had signed Miguel Tejada. His love of baseball and his amazing power-hitting made games at Camden Yards crackle with excitement. Tejada led the league with 150 RBIs in his first season as an Oriole.

LEFT: Eddie Murray
TOP RIGHT: Mike Mussina
BOTTOM RIGHT: Miguel Tejada

EARL SIDNEY WEAVER
BALTIMORE, A.L. 1968-1982, 1985-1986
MANAGED ORIOLES WITH INTE

On the Sidelines

There are many ways to lose a baseball game, and many ways to win one. This is where having a smart manager is important. Some of the brightest minds in baseball have called the Orioles' dugout "home," including Johnny Oates, Frank Robinson, and Davey Johnson.

In 1955, the Orioles hired Paul Richards to manage the team. Richards was a good judge of talent, and an expert at baseball *strategy*. He decided to let Baltimore's young players get experience right away. In 1960, the Orioles had four starting pitchers who were 22 or younger. These four young pitchers won a total of 55 games. Fans nicknamed them Richards's "Baby Birds."

Baltimore's most famous manager was Earl Weaver. He led the team from 1968 to 1982, and again in 1985 and 1986. Weaver believed that the best way to win a game was to get runners on base and send a slugger to the plate. He also believed that studying statistics could give his team an advantage. He must have been right, because he had only one losing season as a manager.

In 1996, Earl Weaver was honored as one of baseball's greatest managers when he entered the Hall of Fame in Cooperstown, New York.

One Great Day

When the fan voting for the 2001 All-Star Game was finished, 40-year-old Cal Ripken Jr. was as surprised as anyone in baseball. He had been chosen as the A.L.'s starting third baseman. Ripken was playing in his final season, and he was batting only .240

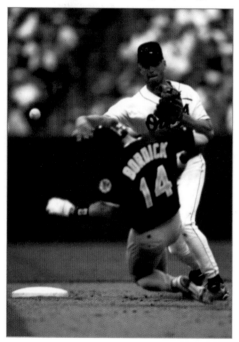

with four home runs. Even so, baseball fans wanted to see him just one more time.

Ripken got an even bigger surprise when he trotted out to his position to start the first inning. Alex Rodriguez walked over to him and shoved him toward his old position at shortstop, where he had once started 12 All-Star games in a row. Rodriguez played third base in his place. A lot of baseball fans had tears in their eyes after this touching *gesture*.

The tears returned two innings later, when Ripken walked to the plate for his first at bat. The fans rose to their feet and gave him a long ovation. No sooner had the crowd quieted down than Ripken slammed

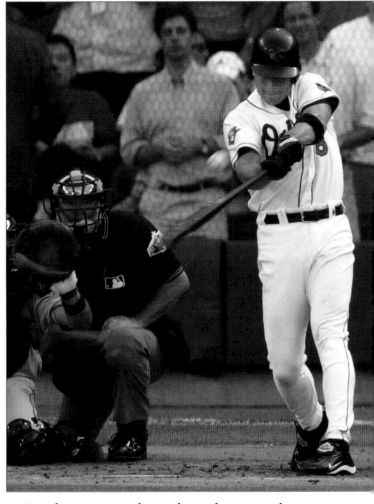

LEFT: Cal Ripken Jr. completes a double play during his days as an All-Star shortstop.
RIGHT: Ripken slugs Chan Ho Park's pitch toward the left field stands in the 2001 All-Star Game.

the first pitch he saw from Chan Ho Park into the left field stands for a home run.

In the sixth inning, Ripken was taken out of the game. Play was stopped while a short *ceremony* was held to honor him. Every player on both teams came out to congratulate him on his great career.

The A.L. went on to win 4–1. Ripken was selected as the game's MVP. He had won the award before, in 1991. No one else in A.L. history had won this honor twice.

"Cal comes up, sees one pitch, and hits a home run off a pitcher he has probably never seen before," said an amazed Randy Johnson, a fellow All-Star. "That's the kind of magic that Cal brings to the field, that he's brought to the field for 20 years."

Legend Has It

Who invented the "pancake" glove?

LEGEND HAS IT that Paul Richards did. The Baltimore manager was tired of watching his catchers miss the **knuckleballs** thrown by his star pitcher, Hoyt Wilhelm. In 1960, he ordered gigantic flat gloves to be made, so that it would be easier to block these dipping, darting pitches. The first "pancake" glove measured almost 16 inches across, and 50 inches in *circumference*. Today, catcher's mitts can be no larger than 38 inches in circumference. In the end, Richards decided to trade Wilhelm to the Chicago White Sox for shortstop Luis Aparicio, who would help the Orioles win their first pennant. "You just don't want a knuckleballer pitching for you," Richards finally admitted. Of course, he added, "You don't want one pitching *against* you, either!"

RIGHT: As this trading card shows, Sammy Stewart's record-breaking start was big news in the baseball world.

Which pitcher got off to the best start in Orioles history?

1978 RECORD BREAKER | SAMMY STEWART
Major League Record: 7 Straight Strikeouts During First Game in Majors

LEGEND HAS IT that Sammy Stewart did. On September 1, 1978, Stewart had just arrived in Baltimore from the minor leagues. He started the Orioles' game against the Chicago White Sox and began throwing 95 mile-per-hour fastballs. Stewart struck out the first batter he faced in the second inning, took a deep breath, and continued to go after the Chicago hitters. One by one, the White Sox walked back to the dugout, shaking their heads, unable to lay a bat on Stewart's pitches. He set a record that day by striking out seven **major leaguers** in a row in his first game.

Who was the hardest-throwing pitcher the Orioles ever signed?

LEGEND HAS IT that it was Steve Dalkowski, whose nickname was "White Lightning." His fastball hissed toward the batter with terrifying speed, but like lightning, you never knew where it would strike. Many experts estimated that Dalkowski threw the ball between 105 and 110 miles per hour. Unfortunately, he could not control his pitches, and the Orioles never called him up from the minor leagues.

It Really Happened

Nothing in baseball is more frustrating than a losing streak. There is simply no explaining how a team with good players can go game after game without winning. At the start of the 1988 season, Baltimore's manager, Cal Ripken Sr., watched his team lose its first six games. Edgar Bennett Williams, the Orioles' owner, replaced Ripken with Frank Robinson. Williams hoped a new leader might help the team win.

Robinson tried every way he knew to get that first victory, but the losing went on and on. The Orioles broke the old record of 13 losses to begin a season, and kept on going. Finally, after losing 21 in a row, the Orioles won their first game—a 9–0 shutout of the Chicago White Sox. "We're not the O's anymore," Robinson joked about the team's nickname. "We're the '1's.'"

Actually, the most embarrassed man in Baltimore that April was not Robinson. That honor belonged to a radio DJ named Mike

Filippelli. After the team's 10th loss, he bet his partner that the Orioles would stop their streak before it reached 13. His price for losing this bet was to become a human ice cream sundae. Filippelli had to sit in a baby pool wearing an Orioles helmet and uniform, while fans who listened to the radio station dumped chocolate syrup, nuts, fruit syrup, and whipped cream on his head. They finished it off with a big cherry!

LEFT: Frank Robinson finally had something to smile about after the team's 22nd game in 1988.   **ABOVE**: Some thought the Orioles' losing streak was funny. Cal Ripken Sr. saw no humor in it.

Team Spirit

Baltimore fans believe that the Orioles belong to the city. When the team is doing well, everyone in town feels like they are part of the success. When the Orioles struggle, Baltimore fans are not afraid to let the team owners know that the club should be playing better.

The Orioles have some of baseball's most loyal and loving fans. The children who watched the Orioles play in the 1960s and 1970s in old Memorial Stadium now bring their own children to games at Camden Yards. They travel from Delaware, Virginia, Maryland, and Washington, D.C.

The Orioles are Baltimore's most famous sports team, and they are a source of great pride for the city. The team's stadium was part of a rebirth of Baltimore's historic waterfront, which also includes a wonderful modern aquarium. Many fans start their day touring this area, and then walk over to Camden Yards to watch the Orioles play.

Cal Ripken Jr. reaches out to the crowd at Camden Yards after setting the record for the most games played in a row.

Timeline

Brooks Robinson jumps for joy after the Orioles win the 1966 World Series.

1902
The St. Louis Browns join the A.L.

1966
The Orioles defeat the Los Angeles Dodgers for their first championship.

1973
Al Bumbry is named A.L. **Rookie of the Year**.

1954
The team moves to Baltimore and becomes the Orioles.

1970
The Orioles beat the Cincinnati Reds for their second championship.

1980
Steve Stone wins the A.L. Cy Young Award.

An early Orioles trading card

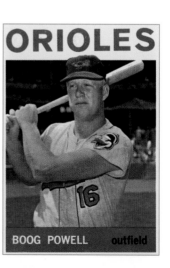

Boog Powell, the 1970 A.L. MVP.

Cal Ripken Jr. is honored as baseball's new "Iron Man."

1985

The Orioles hit seven home runs in a game against the California Angels.

1995

Cal Ripken Jr. sets a new record when he plays in his 2,131st game in a row.

1983

The Orioles defeat the Philadelphia Phillies for their third championship.

1992

Oriole Park at Camden Yards opens.

2004

Melvin Mora bats .340 for a new Orioles record.

Jim Palmer fires a pitch in the 1983 World Series.

Melvin Mora

Fun Facts

FIRST AND FOREMOST

In 1996, Brady Anderson set a record when he led off four games in a row with a home run.

NOW CAN I STAY UP LATE?

When second baseman Brian Roberts was a child, one of his babysitters was a college baseball player named B.J. Surhoff. In 2003, they became teammates on the Orioles.

FOUR ACES

In 1971, the Orioles had four 20-game winners on their pitching staff. Dave McNally won 21 games, and Mike Cuellar, Jim Palmer, and Pat Dobson each won 20.

SWISH

Tim Stoddard, a relief pitcher for the Orioles in the 1970s and 1980s, was a member of the 1974 North Carolina State University basketball squad. The team won the national championship that year.

ABOVE: Brady Anderson
TOP RIGHT: The Ripkens: Billy, Cal Sr., and Cal Jr.
BOTTOM RIGHT: Bobby Grich

LIKE FATHER, LIKE SONS

In 1987, Cal Ripken Sr. was the manager of the Orioles. His sons—second baseman Billy and shortstop Cal Jr.—made up his double-play combination.

ONE-YEAR WONDERS

In 1901, the A.L. had a team in Milwaukee called the Brewers. They finished last and lost a lot of money. This was the club that the league moved to St. Louis in 1902 and renamed the Browns.

SOLID GOLD

The Orioles have had six players who won four or more Gold Gloves for their great fielding—third baseman Brooks Robinson, shortstop Mark Belanger, outfielder Paul Blair, second baseman Bobby Grich, and pitchers Jim Palmer and Mike Mussina. Robinson won the most, with 16.

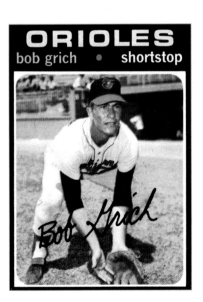

ORIOLES
bob grich • shortstop

Talking Baseball

"You are challenged by the game of baseball to do your very best day in and day out. That's all I've ever tried to do."
—*Cal Ripken Jr., on what made him so good from game to game*

"I had one goal and I was allowed to pursue it. My folks always made sure I had a new glove and a good pair of spikes…it was a nice feeling."
—*Paul Blair, on following his dream of being a baseball player*

"Baseball is pitching, three-run homers, and fundamentals."
—*Earl Weaver, on the three most important parts of the game*

"I always tried to do the best. I knew I couldn't always *be* the best, but I *tried* to be."

—*Frank Robinson, on what made him great*

"Baseball always has been my favorite sport since we went to Williamsport."

—*Boog Powell, on the thrill of playing in the 1955 Little League World Series*

"The player's bat is what speaks loudest when it's contract time, but there are moments when the glove has the last word."

—*Brooks Robinson, on the value of fielding*

LEFT: Cal Ripken Jr.
ABOVE: Boog Powell, Brooks Robinson, and Frank Robinson

For the Record

T he great Orioles teams and players have left their marks on the record books. These are the "best of the best"…

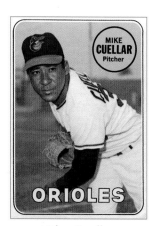

Mike Cuellar

Jim Palmer

ORIOLES AWARD WINNERS

WINNER	AWARD	YEAR
Roy Sievers	Rookie of the Year	1949*
Ron Hansen	Rookie of the Year	1960
Brooks Robinson	Most Valuable Player	1964
Curt Blefary	Rookie of the Year	1965
Brooks Robinson	All-Star Game MVP	1966
Frank Robinson	Most Valuable Player	1966
Frank Robinson	World Series MVP	1966
Mike Cuellar	Cy Young Award	1969
Boog Powell	Most Valuable Player	1970
Brooks Robinson	World Series MVP	1970
Frank Robinson	All-Star Game MVP	1971
Jim Palmer	Cy Young Award	1973
Al Bumbry	Rookie of the Year	1973
Jim Palmer	Cy Young Award	1975
Jim Palmer	Cy Young Award	1976
Eddie Murray	Rookie of the Year	1977
Mike Flanagan	Cy Young Award	1979
Steve Stone	Cy Young Award	1980
Cal Ripken Jr.	Rookie of the Year	1982
Cal Ripken Jr.	Most Valuable Player	1983
Rick Dempsey	World Series MVP	1983
Gregg Olson	Rookie of the Year	1989
Frank Robinson	Manager of the Year	1989
Cal Ripken Jr.	Most Valuable Player	1991
Cal Ripken Jr.	All-Star Game MVP	1991
Davey Johnson	Manager of the Year	1997
Roberto Alomar	All-Star Game MVP	1998
Cal Ripken Jr.	All-Star Game MVP	2001
Miguel Tejada	All-Star Game MVP	2005

*Team played as St. Louis Browns

ORIOLES ACHIEVEMENTS

ACHIEVEMENT	YEAR
A.L. Pennant Winner	1944*
A.L. Pennant Winner	1966
World Series Champions	1966
A.L. East Champions	1969
A.L. Pennant Winner	1969
A.L. East Champions	1970
A.L. Pennant Winner	1970
World Series Champions	1970
A.L. East Champions	1971
A.L. Pennant Winner	1971
A.L. East Champions	1973
A.L. East Champions	1974
A.L. East Champions	1979
A.L. Pennant Winner	1979
A.L. East Champions	1983
A.L. Pennant Winner	1983
World Series Champions	1983
A.L. East Champions	1997

Team played as St. Louis Browns

F. ROBINSON • H. BAUER • B. ROBINSON

THE CHAMPS

LEFT: Roberto Alomar, the 1998 All-Star Game MVP.
TOP RIGHT: Mike Cuellar and Brooks Robinson celebrate the team's 1970 championship.
BOTTOM RIGHT: Frank Robinson, Hank Bauer, and Brooks Robinson

Pinpoints

The history of a baseball team is made up of many smaller stories. These stories take place all over the map—not just in the city a team calls "home." Match the push-pins on these maps to the Team Facts and you will begin to see the story of the Orioles unfold!

TEAM FACTS

1 Baltimore, Maryland—*The team has played here since 1954.*

2 New York, New York—*Jim Palmer was born here.*

3 Euclid, Ohio—*Steve Stone was born here.*

4 Billings, Montana—*Dave McNally was born here.*

5 Inglewood, California—*Scott McGregor was born here.*

6 St. Louis, Missouri—*The team played here as the Browns from 1902 to 1953.*

7 Little Rock, Arkansas—*Brooks Robinson was born here.*

8 Beaumont, Texas—*Frank Robinson was born here.*

9 Lakeland, Florida—*Boog Powell was born here.*

10 Navan, Ontario, Canada—*Erik Bedard was born here.*

11 Havana, Cuba—*Rafael Palmeiro was born here.*

12 Agua Negras, Venezuela—*Melvin Mora was born here.*

Rafael Palmeiro

Play Ball

Baseball is a game played between two teams over nine innings. Teams take one turn at bat and one turn in the field during each inning. A turn at bat ends when three outs are made. The batters on the hitting team try to reach base safely. The players on the fielding team try to prevent this from happening.

In baseball, the ball is controlled by the pitcher. The pitcher must throw the ball to the batter, who decides whether or not to swing at each pitch. If a batter swings and misses, it is a strike. If the batter lets a good pitch go by, it is also a strike. If the batter swings and the ball does not stay in fair territory (between the v-shaped lines that begin at home plate) it is called "foul," and is counted as a strike. If the pitcher throws three strikes, the batter is out. If the pitcher throws four bad pitches before that, the batter is awarded first base. This is called a base-on-balls, or "walk."

When the batter swings the bat and hits the ball, everyone springs into action. If a fielder catches a batted ball before it hits the ground, the batter is out. If a fielder scoops the ball off the ground and throws it to first base before the batter arrives, the batter is out. If the batter reaches first base safely, he is credited with a hit. A one-base hit is called a single, a two-base hit is called a double, a three-base hit is called a triple, and a four-base hit is called a home run.

Runners who reach base are only safe when they are touching one of the bases. If they are caught between the bases, the fielders can tag them with the ball and record an out.

A batter who is able to circle the bases and make it back to home plate before three outs are made is credited with a run scored. The team with the most runs after nine innings is the winner.

Anyone who has played baseball (or softball) knows that it can be a complicated game. Every player on the field has a job to do. Different players have different strengths and weaknesses. The pitchers, batters, and managers make hundreds of decisions every game. The more you play and watch baseball, the more "little things" you are likely to notice. The next time you are at a game, look for these plays:

PLAY LIST

DOUBLE PLAY—A play where the fielding team is able to make two outs on one batted ball. This usually happens when a runner is on first base, and the batter hits a ground ball to one of the infielders. The base runner is forced out at second base and the ball is then thrown to first base before the batter arrives.

HIT AND RUN—A play where the runner on first base sprints to second base while the pitcher is throwing the ball to the batter. When the second baseman or shortstop moves toward the base to wait for the catcher's throw, the batter tries to hit the ball to the place that the fielder has just left. If the batter swings and misses, the fielding team can tag the runner out.

INTENTIONAL WALK—A play when the pitcher throws four bad pitches on purpose, allowing the batter to walk to first base. This happens when the pitcher would much rather face the next batter—and is willing to risk putting a runner on base.

SACRIFICE BUNT—A play where the batter makes an out on purpose so that a teammate can move to the next base. On a bunt, the batter tries to "deaden" the pitch with the bat instead of swinging at it.

SHOESTRING CATCH—A play where an outfielder catches a short hit an inch or two above the ground, near the tops of his shoes. It is not easy to run as fast as you can and lower your glove without slowing down. It can be risky, too. If a fielder misses a shoestring catch, the ball might roll all the way to the fence.

Glossary

ALL-STARS—Players who are selected to play in baseball's annual All-Star Game.

AMERICAN LEAGUE (A.L.)—One of baseball's two major leagues. The A.L. started play in 1901. The National League began play in 1876.

AMERICAN LEAGUE CHAMPIONSHIP SERIES (ALCS)—The competition that has decided the American League pennant since 1969.

COMPLETE GAME—A statistic credited to a pitcher who stays in a game from start to finish.

CY YOUNG AWARD—The trophy given to each league's best pitcher each year.

FUNDAMENTALS—The basic skills of baseball.

GOLD GLOVE—An award given each year to baseball's best fielders.

GRAND SLAM—A home run with the bases loaded.

KNUCKLEBALLS—Pitches thrown with no spin, which "wobble" as they near home plate. A knuckleball is held with the tips of the fingers, so the batter sees a pitcher's knuckles when he throws it.

LINEUP—The list of players who are playing in a game.

MAJOR LEAGUERS—Players who belong to a team in the American or National League, which make up the major leagues.

MINOR-LEAGUE—Belonging to one of the professional baseball leagues at a lower level than the major leagues.

MOST VALUABLE PLAYER (MVP)—An award given each year to each league's top player; an MVP is also selected for the World Series and All-Star Game.

NATIONAL LEAGUE (N.L.)—The older of the two major leagues. The N.L. started play in 1876.

PENNANT—A league championship. The term comes from the triangular flag awarded to each season's champion, beginning in the 1870s.

RELIEF PITCHER—A pitcher who is brought into a game to replace another pitcher. Relief pitchers can be seen warming up in the bullpen.

ROOKIE OF THE YEAR—An annual award given to each league's best first-year player.

RUNS BATTED IN (RBIs)—A statistic that measures the number of runners a batter drives home.

SHUT OUT—Did not allow an opponent to score. A game won in this way is called a "shutout."

SLUGGERS—Powerful hitters.

STANDINGS—A daily list of teams, starting with the team with the best record and ending with the team with the worst record.

SWITCH-HITTER—A player who can hit from either side of home plate. Switch-hitters bat left-handed against right-handed pitchers, and right-handed against left-handed pitchers.

TRIPLE CROWN—An honor given to a player who leads the league in home runs, batting average, and RBIs.

WORLD SERIES—The world championship series played between the winners of the American and National Leagues.

OTHER WORDS TO KNOW

CEREMONY—An act to honor a special occasion.

CIRCUMFERENCE—The distance around an object.

DECADES—Periods of ten years; also specific periods, such as the 1950s.

EVAPORATE—Disappear, or turn into vapor.

FEISTY—Tough and competitive.

FLANNEL—A soft wool or cotton material.

GESTURE—An action meant to show feeling for someone.

LOGO—A symbol or design that represents a company or team.

STRATEGY—A plan to win or succeed.

SYNTHETIC—Made in a laboratory, not in nature.

TRADITION—A belief or custom that is handed down from generation to generation.

Places to Go

ON THE ROAD

BALTIMORE ORIOLES
Oriole Park at Camden Yards
333 West Camden Street
Baltimore, Maryland 21201
(888) 848-2473

**NATIONAL BASEBALL
HALL OF FAME AND MUSEUM**
25 Main Street
Cooperstown, New York 13326
(888) 425-5633
www.baseballhalloffame.org

ON THE WEB

THE BALTIMORE ORIOLES   www.Orioles.com
 • *to learn more about the Orioles*

MAJOR LEAGUE BASEBALL   www.mlb.com
 • *to learn about all the major league teams*

MINOR LEAGUE BASEBALL   www.minorleaguebaseball.com
 • *to learn more about the minor leagues*

ON THE BOOKSHELVES

To learn more about the sport of baseball, look for these books at your library or bookstore:

 • Kelly, James. *Baseball.* New York, NY: DK, 2005.

 • Jacobs, Greg. *The Everything Kids' Baseball Book.* Cincinnati, OH: Adams Media Corporation, 2006.

 • Stewart, Mark and Kennedy, Mike. *Long Ball: The Legend and Lore of the Home Run.* Minneapolis, MN: Millbrook Press, 2006.

Index

PAGE NUMBERS IN **BOLD** REFER TO ILLUSTRATIONS.

Alomar, Roberto 9, **9**, 40, **41**
Anderson, Brady..................9, 36, **36**
Aparacio, Luis..................7, 28
Barber, Steve 7, 37
Bauer, Hank..................16, **41**
Bedard, Erik..................11, 43
Belanger, Mark..................37
Blair, Paul..................7, 37, 38
Blefary, Curt..................40
Boddicker, Mike..................18
Browns, St. Louis 6, 7, 20, 34, 37, 40, 41, 43
Bumbry, Al 34, 40
Bunker, Wally..................7, 17
Clift, Harlond 6
Cuellar, Mike..................36, 40, **40**, **41**
Dalkowski, Steve..................29
Decker, Hal..................14
Dempsey, Rick..................18, **19**, 40
Dobson, Pat..................36
Drabowsky, Moe..................16
Drysdale, Don 16
Erickson, Scott 9
Etchebarren, Andy **17**
Filippelli, Mike..................31
Flanagan, Mike..................18, 22, 40
Fregosi, Jim..................37
Grich, Bobby..................37, **37**
Hansen, Ron 40
Hartzell, Jim..................14
Johnson, Davey..................25, 40
Johnson, Randy..................27
Koufax, Sandy..................16, 17
Loes, Billy..................**14**
Miller, Stu..................37
Markakis, Nick..................**4**, 11
Martinez, Tippy..................18
McGregor, Scott..................18, 43
McNally, Dave..................7, 17, **17**, 18, 36, 43
Memorial Stadium 13, 33
Mora, Melvin..................**10**, 23, 35, **35**, 43
Murray, Eddie..................9, 22, **22**, 40

Mussina, Mike..................9, 23, **23**, 37
Myers, Randy..................9
Oates, Johnny..................25
Olson, Gregg..................40
Oriole Park at Camden Yards 9, **12**, 13, 23, **32**, 33, 35
Palmeiro, Rafael 9, 43, **43**
Palmer, Jim 7, 17, 18, 21, **35**, 36, 37, 40, **40**, 43
Pappas, Milt..................7
Park, Chan Ho..................27
Patterson, Corey..................**15**
Powell, Boog 7, 16, **17**, **34**, 39, **39**, 40, 43
Pratt, Del..................6
Richards, Paul..................25, 28
Ripken, Billy 37, **37**
Ripken, Cal, Jr...................**8**, 9, 22, 26, **26**, 27, **27**, **32**, 35, **35**, 37, **37**, 38, **38**, 40
Ripken, Cal, Sr...................30, **31**, 37, **37**
Roberts, Brian **4**, **10**, 11, 36
Robinson, Brooks..................7, **7**, 16, **17**, 18, **18**, 21, 21, **34**, 37, 39, **39**, 40, **41**, 43
Robinson, Frank..................7, 16, **16**, 21, **21**, 25, 30, **30**, 39, **39**, 40, **41**, 43
Rodriguez, Alex..................26
Ruth, Babe..................13
Sievers, Roy..................40
Sisler, George 6, 20, **20**
Stewart, Sammy..................29, **29**
Stoddard, Tim..................36
Stone, Steve..................34, 40, 43
Surhoff, B.J...................36
Tejada, Miguel 23, **23**, 40
Tobin, Jack..................6
Wallace, Bobby..................6, **6**
Walsh, Stan 14
Weaver, Earl..................7, **24**, 25, 38
Wilhelm, Hoyt..................28
Williams, Edgar Bennett..................30
Williams, Ken..................6, 20

The Team

MARK STEWART has written more than 25 books on baseball, and over 100 sports books for kids. He grew up in New York City during the 1960s rooting for the Yankees and Mets, and now takes his two daughters, Mariah and Rachel, to the same ball-parks. Mark comes from a family of writers. His grand-father was Sunday Editor of the *New York Times* and his mother was Articles Editor of *Ladies' Home Journal* and *McCall's*. Mark has profiled hundreds of athletes over the last 20 years. He has also written several books about his native New York and New Jersey, his home today. Mark is a graduate of Duke University, with a degree in history. He lives with his daughters and wife, Sarah, overlooking Sandy Hook, NJ.

JAMES L. GATES, JR. has served as Library Director at the National Baseball Hall of Fame since 1995. He had previously served in academic libraries for almost fifteen years. He holds degrees from Belmont Abbey College, the University of Notre Dame, and Indiana University. During his career Jim has authored several aca-demic articles and has served in an editorial capacity on multiple book, mag-azine, and museum publications, and he also serves as host for the Annual Cooperstown Symposium on Baseball and American Culture. He is an ardent Baltimore Orioles fan and enjoys watching baseball with his wife and two children.